Bill Putnam taught for many years at Bournemouth University as Principal Lecturer in Archaeology. He has now retired, but continues to lecture widely to appreciative audiences on Dorset's archaeology. He is Chairman of Wessex Archaeology, the major professional archaeological unit in the south-west of England. He has also written *Roman Dorset*, which continues the story of Dorset from the end of this book.

Following page
A gold plate from the Clandon Barrow. The plate is 6 inches long, and was probably sewn onto a cloak or piece of clothing (see page 38).

DISCOVER DORSET

THE PREHISTORIC AGE

BILL PUTNAM

THE DOVECOTE PRESS

A Victorian engraving of the opening of a Bronze Age
barrow at Shapwick, near Wimborne. The occasional
presence of gold in such barrows led to great damage in
the nineteenth century.

First published in 1998 by The Dovecote Press Ltd
Stanbridge, Wimborne, Dorset BH21 4JD

ISBN 1 874336 62 8

Series designed by Humphrey Stone

Typeset in Sabon by The Typesetting Bureau
Wimborne, Dorset
Printed and bound by Baskerville Press, Salisbury, Wiltshire

A CIP catalogue record for this book is available
from the British Library

1 3 5 7 9 8 6 4 2

CONTENTS

INTRODUCTION

Prehistory means literally before history; that is to say the period before people began to write their words down and perhaps leave them for historians to read today. This moment for Britain is the middle of the first century BC, and this is a crucial stage in the process of studying our ancestors.

After that there are people with whom we can fairly easily identify, i.e. the Romans. They had roads, houses, cities, disciplined armies, poetry, sports, parliaments, emperors and even historians. Limited though the original Roman historical writing is for Britain, nevertheless we can read what Julius Caesar himself wrote when he briefly conquered southern Britain in 55-54 BC, even though we must take it with a pinch of salt.

But before that point in time it is a very different problem. Give or take a short period when Roman traders were visiting Britain, we know no names, no thoughts, no heroes, no cities, no political scenarios, no priest, no commoner, no king.

It is hardly surprising that the methods of studying prehistory are very different from the familiar techniques of history. Modern historians compare different versions of the Battle of Britain, according to which side of the war they view it from.

In prehistory you will have no version at all to study. You will be lucky if you even know there has been a war. Even if physical evidence of battle occurs such as a burial site of those who died, you may well not know the participants, the causes or the outcome.

An aerial photograph of Knowlton Rings, near Cranborne, one of the most remarkable and enigmatic prehistoric sites in the county. The two great Neolithic henges (centre, and encircling the farm buildings top right), together with their associated Bronze Age barrows and other circular features show clearly. The ruins of a medieval church lie within the best preserved of the two henges, adding to Knowlton's atmosphere.

[7]

What's the point then? Dr Johnson in a memorable comment said 'All that is really known of the ancient state of Britain is contained in a few pages. We can know no more than what the old writers have told us.' But this is far from true.

Firstly we must look at the full span of human history. All of this story is important to us. We now know something of the remote origins of the human race, and it lies in Africa over three million years ago. The story of western civilisation, the common material of school history books, important though it is, forms only the very recent phase of an immense and moving story of the human race's rise to dominance in this world.

By far the longest part of the story occurs before written records began, and though development was slow, this story is the basis of everything we can know about ourselves.

Many prehistorians are scientists to some degree or other. This is not surprising, since our new knowledge of prehistory comes very much from scientific methods used in archaeological research. It does not, however, follow that to understand prehistory you must have a deep scientific knowledge. Far from it. The penultimate chapter of this book will provide you with the necessary background. Without the experts we would not know these things, but once the research has been done, the information, interpreted for the layman, is available for all to study.

Often the work is done by scientists with little understanding of the consequences for our interpretation of prehistory. The key figure is the person who can grasp the scientific data and see its application to a further stage in the understanding of human development.

What can we know of people in prehistoric times? Most evidence relates to the way ordinary people lived (oddly enough the very thing it is difficult to find information about for some more recent periods).

Pottery, tools, personal adornments, homes and weapons speak of ordinary people. Alas, the need to defend oneself was as prominent then as in life today. At a different level there are structures which speak of organisation, of political, religious and military power. These are to be seen in the hillforts of the Iron Age, the splendours of the great stone monuments like Stonehenge, the serried ranks of impressive burial mounds along the South Dorset Ridgeway.

But as you ask yourself the exact significance of each of these monuments, the problem reveals itself; how ever many holes we dig or microscopes we peer down, we can never ever know what the builders of these monuments thought, what their aims were, whether they succeeded. These mysteries will remain closed to us. There are as many interpretations of Stonehenge as there are people who have studied it. Your interpretation is as valid as any. But, and it is an important but, such interpretations are only valid provided that they take account of what has been discovered in the ground or through scientific study.

It is legitimate to fill in unknown detail to present a complete and coherent and logical hypothesis. It is not legitimate to fantasise a solution which ignores factors which are known for certain from archaeological research. In Britain there is a thriving lunatic fringe in archaeology. This is their problem; they ignore research and base their theories on myth, legend and their own imagination, rather than the evidence. It is extraordinary how many people in Britain still think Stonehenge was the major temple of the Druids in Caesar's time, following the ideas of William Stukeley who peopled the monument with Druids, ignoring the scientific and indisputable dating which places Stonehenge and the Druids two millennia apart.

Applying these rules of evidence, I hope that the rest of this book will give a coherent account of the story of human activity in Dorset, before the Roman army arrived in 43 AD and, among their other activities, started to write things down.

PEOPLES, PERIODS AND PLACES

We are talking of events a very long time ago indeed. Creatures distinct from the apes, though hardly identifiable as human, first appeared on earth something like 4,000,000 years ago. By the time this book appears in print this figure will probably have been revised!

They appeared in Africa, and the debate on what triggered the change is not one to go into here. They are known about because in places like Tanzania there are rocks which enclosed and petrified their bones, and which have been brought to view by water erosion. Much is made of this evidence and every day we can read of the latest theories of which creature descended from which, and perhaps more importantly to the creatures themselves, which ate which.

It should always be remembered that the evidence available is a very tiny fraction of the evidence which is buried in the rocks. We are only just beginning to understand about it at all.

Amazing claims are made based on the shape of the bones and the scientific study of DNA. But do not be in too much of a hurry to believe all you read on this topic. The main purpose of such publications can often be to impress the bodies which fund the research, and to ensure employment for the following year. In such circumstances a large pinch of salt is often necessary.

As far as Britain is concerned, early humans appear about 500,000 years ago. Not that you would have recognised Britain, still less Dorset, that long ago. The island we know today is the result of climate, weathering and ice. Britain was not even an island till about 6,000 BC, when the sea broke through to form the English Channel.

These first 'Britons' were definitely not the *homo sapiens sapiens* we know today. They are classified mainly as *homo erectus* and some as *homo sapiens neanderthalensis*. The battle still rages as to their exact relationship to one another.

We call this period the Palaeolithic Age, from the Greek words for 'old' and 'stone'. Archaeologists subdivide this into the Lower Palaeolithic and the Upper Palaeolithic. The Lower came first. For Britain, the Upper, with the arrival of *homo sapiens sapiens*, happened soon after 15,000 BC, though it was considerably earlier in Europe, particularly France.

It is difficult for us to find out much about the Lower Palaeolithic. The reason is that geological processes have destroyed much of the evidence. Deep ice has covered the land. At other times warm rivers flowing from the ice cap swept all before them. The ice ages which cover the last half a million years in Britain are a complex subject, which is also constantly under new study.

Suffice to say that the sole evidence of the Palaeolithic in Dorset is the finding of the stone hand axes which represent the main tools of Palaeolithic humans. These are crude tools, but along with the wooden weapons and tools which we do not find, they made life possible. Flint provided sharp edges.

None of these tools are found where they were dropped, but rather swept miles away by ice and rivers. They frequently appear in river terrace gravels. It was only in the nineteenth century that they were recognised as human tools at all. A favourite explanation had been that they were the result of lightning strikes, or they were 'elfin thunderbolts'.

But in recent years one place has been found in Britain, not all that far from Dorset, where there is a land surface still in place though deeply buried, where humans actually trod 500,000 years ago. This is Boxgrove in West Sussex, not far from Chichester.

In many ways this has been the most important excavation in Britain this century. A beach existed here, at the foot of a cliff. Humans came to its comparative shelter to knap flints to make axes (they were surprisingly good at it). Material weathered from the cliff above gradually buried the land surface so deeply that it only emerged in modern quarrying operations. Not only are there flint axes lying where they were originally dropped, but there is the debris of flint knapping which even reveals where the knapper was kneeling as he or she made the axe. There are bones of the animals they ate. And most dramatic of all, part of a human shin bone and two teeth. The excavators have hoped, without success so far, for skull fragments to show what these earliest Britons looked like. Two teeth do not get you very far in this respect.

The following table gives some idea of the timescale we are dealing with, and order of the prehistoric periods as we define them. Note that the scale changes from one side of the table to the other.

TIMELINE FOR PREHISTORIC BRITAIN			
YEARS AGO		YEARS BC	
500,000	Lower Palaeolithic First humans in Britain		
		9,000	Mesolithic
400,000			
		4,000	Neolithic
300,000			
		2,000	Bronze Age
200,000			
		700	Iron Age
100,000			
		43 AD	Roman conquest
15,000	Upper Palaeolithic begins		

HUNTERS AND GATHERERS

THE LOWER PALAEOLITHIC

During the enormous time span of the Lower Palaeolithic, people appeared in Britain from time to time. In geological terms this is the Pleistocene period. The climate changed frequently.

Geologists talk of glacials and interglacials. During the glacials ice sheets spread south from the northern ice cap and covered most of Britain. It was during such activity that our present landscape was gradually sculpted, partly by the moving ice itself, and partly by the flows of water that followed when the ice melted.

When so much water was stored in the ice, the level of the sea dropped by as much as 100 metres (110 yards) and there was no water between Britain and the mainland. Only a few humans ventured as far north as Britain, and then only into the southern part where the ice had not completely covered the land. Vegetation was scarce and animals to hunt were rare. There were mammoths, reindeer, horses and other animals that could survive such conditions.

In the interglacials the temperature rose, the ice melted, and Britain was an island. Archaeologists have found the bones of elephant and hippopotamus, with lions, hyenas, bison and deer. Extensive forests grew. Visits by humans were more frequent. But with the rare exception of such sites as Boxgrove, the evidence we find is only the flint hand axes displayed in many museums.

People lived in the open, except where natural caves provided shelter, though these are rare in southern Britain. Those in the Mendips are the nearest to Dorset. Probably they followed the herds of wild animals on which their survival depended. Where possible they gathered wild plants as food, though the further north they went, the more difficult this became.

Their stone tools have been much studied both here and on the continent. This in not surprising as they are frequently the only

Flint axes from the Palaeolithic period.

evidence available. It is too complex a subject for detailed description here, but there are many books on the topic. Four major types are known after places where they were first recognised and researched.

The earliest were the Clactonian tools, named after a rich site found at Clacton in Essex. The majority of these are crude flakes struck from large flints. Next came the Acheulian industries with multi-purpose core hand-axes, and small cutting and scraping tools made from the flakes. Acheulian tools were found near the oldest human skull fragments found at Britain at Swanscombe in Kent. These were some 250,000 years old. (Perhaps one day much older skull fragments will be found at Boxgrove.) Levallois tools were largely flake tools struck from carefully prepared flint cores. There is a site at Northfleet in Kent where large numbers were made. The final Lower Palaeolithic tools made in Britain are known as the Mousterian industry. These are also flake tools with one flattened end.

There were few humans in Britain during the last glacial, known to the geologists as the Devensian. Sometime after 15,000 BC this phase ended, the ice gradually retreated, and Britain entered the warmer interglacial that we enjoy at the present time, the Flandrian.

It remains to be seen whether the human race has interfered so much in the climate that the sequence of glacials and interglacials is now broken.

Thus 15,000 BC saw the real start of the progress to modern humans. The people who came to Britain then were for the first time *homo sapiens sapiens*, fully developed modern human beings. They had been on the continent since about 40,000 BC.

There is evidence for their activity in caves from Wookey Hole in Somerset to Creswell Crags in Derbyshire. (For Dorset there are only the flint tools they accidentally lost.) They were clothed in animal furs, and they wore ornaments in the form of necklaces made from animal teeth and shells. Their stone tools were of excellent quality, and are usually referred to as Cresswellian after the Derbyshire site. Investigation of the caves there continues at the present time.

They made sharp blades from flakes with one side blunted for handling, together with leaf shaped spear points and many other small tools made from flakes. There are two pieces of animal bone from Derbyshire with scratched pictures on them. They are nothing to get excited about but they are the oldest art in Britain! One shows the head of a horse very effectively drawn, and the other a rather ungainly human figure. No such items survive from Dorset.

Of course this is the period at which astounding pictures were painted in caves in France and Spain. No cave art has been found in Britain.

THE MESOLITHIC PERIOD

Between 15,000 BC and about 8,500 BC Upper Palaeolithic humans hunted in the still chilly conditions. The ground was frozen at all times deep down, warming only at the surface during the summer.

The real change came somewhere about 8,500 BC when there was a marked rise in temperature and the ground thawed out. Birch forest began to cover much of Britain, including the chalk uplands of Dorset. This development is well understood, as the plant pollen surviving in peat bogs enables scientists to follow the gradual arrival of new species.

By degrees the birch was replaced by pine forest, and then by hazel and mixed forests of lime, elm and oak. By 5,000 BC, Britain was even warmer than today, by 1 or 2 degrees Celsius. This is known as the Atlantic period in terms of climate.

As more ice melted, sea level rose. But as fast as land close to the sea was submerged, so new areas became available for hunting inland as it got warmer. Britain was fast heading for its present shape on the map.

About 6,000 BC the land bridge which still joined Britain to the continent at the Straits of Dover was finally broken and Britain was permanently an island. There are still shallow places in the Channel and the North Sea, such as the Goodwin Sands, and these are the last traces of the solid land which existed there not so long ago.

Not surprisingly the pattern of human activity altered, sufficiently for archaeologists to need to use a new label. We call the period from 8,500 to 4,000 BC the Mesolithic, meaning Middle Stone Age. Essentially people were still in the hunting and gathering stage, but a lot had changed. The label Maglemosian is often used for these people, after a site in Denmark.

Herds of large animals on migration were replaced by smaller animals living in the forests, particularly deer, wild pig and cattle. Rivers and lakes were full of fish and the sea shore abounded in molluscs. Life was undoubtedly easier than it had been in the Palaeolithic.

The main body of evidence is still flint tools, but these have changed completely. They are classed as microliths, that is to say they are mostly very small sharp flakes, typically 1 to 3 centimetres long (up to 1 inch). Resin was used to glue one or more microliths into wooden or bone handles to make composite tools. Bows and arrows were used, and some have been found in bogs in Denmark. The arrows had very small flint tips.

There were also the earliest examples of axes specially designed to cut down trees, and there is some evidence that land was cleared, though crops were not yet being grown.

Many such flints have been found in Dorset. Oddly, during the excavation of the Dewlish Roman villa near Dorchester, several hundred microliths were found together with the waste created in making them. The villa site is close to the River Develish, and there

Flint tools from the Mesolithic period in Dorset. The two upper flints are cores, from which the very small sharp points were struck.

may well have been a lake here, by the side of which Mesolithic folk camped for fishing long before the Romans came.

Now at last we have human settlement sites identified in Dorset. The best known is on Portland, where excavations over many years have yielded evidence of a long term Mesolithic settlement using microlith tools and larger stone picks for grubbing up roots. Their diet included many molluscs, the shells of which formed large mounds or middens. In fact such shell middens are the commonest indicator of Mesolithic sites in coastal areas.

There are several other Mesolithic sites on the coast, using the sea as their main food source, including several along the Fleet. A major study has been made of Cranborne Chase in this period, which shows that many sites existed on the clay-with-flints which lies on the southward facing slopes on the chalk uplands. Some, but fewer, settlements were found in the river valleys to the south, and the greensand to the north. Many casual finds of Mesolithic flints have been made in almost all parts of Dorset. The problem in visualising Mesolithic settlement is that we do not know whether any of these represent permanent habitation sites, or whether all are temporary hunting camps.

There is no sign of continuity between these sites and the Neolithic period which was to follow. We know remarkably little about the Mesolithic people, partly because little excavation has taken place in Dorset, and partly because we have not found burials, which tell us so much about the later periods of prehistory.

To gain some understanding of Mesolithic settlement, it is necessary to read about the spectacular waterlogged site of Starr Carr in Yorkshire. Here a platform had been built of birch wood on the shore of a lake to provide a firm base for their campsite. They caught and ate several varieties of deer, together with pigs. They kept dogs, which they surely used for hunting. Smaller animals like hares and foxes were caught, and they were probably important for their fur. In addition to their flint tools they used a wide variety of antler and bone for tools, including pins for clothing. There were even beads made from amber, and a wooden paddle suggesting that they had canoes. No canoes were actually found, but dug-out canoes have been found in Britain from this period, for example at Friarton in Perthshire. This was the quiet beginning of British seafaring.

To know whether sites like Starr Carr existed in Dorset must await future research.

THE FIRST FARMERS

Somewhere about 4,000 BC changes began which ultimately were to lead to modern Dorset. People learnt how to farm.

First they began to keep animals rather than hunt them in the wild. Secondly they sowed crops deliberately and harvested them, rather than gather plants in the wild. Tools were still of wood and stone, so we call them the people of the New Stone Age, or using the Greek words for 'new' and 'stone', the Neolithic people.

It's not difficult to see how this change might have happened. Suppose several wild sheep were caught at once in a successful hunt. If they were all slaughtered, the meat might have been unusable long before it was all eaten. Someone had the idea of keeping some of the

A pot of the earliest Neolithic farmers - the first pottery to be made in Britain. The deer antler was used to dig the chalk in the construction of the long barrows and other monuments.

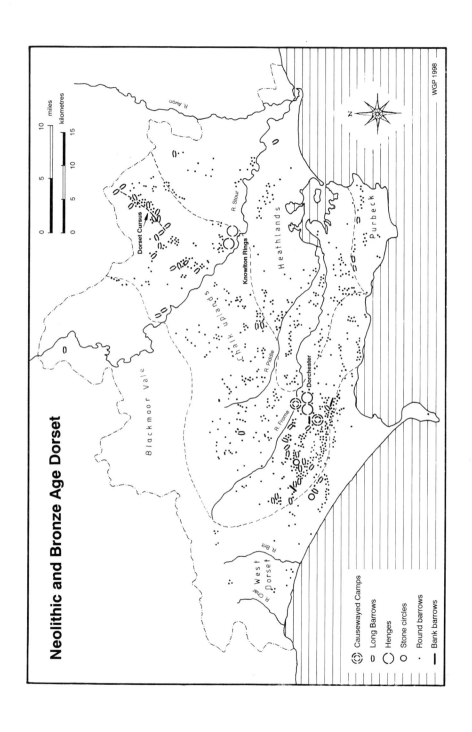

Neolithic and Bronze Age Dorset

Causewayed Camps
Long Barrows
Henges
Stone circles
Round barrows
Bank barrows

R Avon

Dorset Cursus

R Stour

Knowlton Rings

Blackmoor Vale

Chalk uplands

Heathlands

Purbeck

R Piddle

R Frome

Dorchester

R Brit

West Dorset

R Char

miles
kilometres

N

WGP 1998

animals alive and building a fence to keep them in. Then mutton was available to order. It would only be a short step to a breeding flock.

Similarly, seeds of wild emmer (an early sort of wheat) fell to the ground by the back door when the plants which had been laboriously collected were brought in. The next spring, new plants sprang up. It's a short step to deliberate sowing of the seed in an enclosure built to keep animals out.

It is unlikely (though not impossible) that this happened to the Middle Stone Age people independently in southern Britain. It certainly happened in the Middle East, where suitable wild animals and plants were available, and the ideas probably spread across Europe. It may well have happened independently in other parts of the world, such as North and South America and China.

It used to be thought that this, as with most other changes in the way people lived, involved violent invasion by those with the new ideas or the new technology. However, ideas can spread without necessarily entailing an invasion. The most likely explanation, at least for southern Britain, is that small numbers of families carrying with them domestic animals and seeds crossed the Channel early in the fourth millennium BC (Britain was by then an island). They may have fought the indigenous peoples, but may equally have negotiated the use of unoccupied land for their new way of life. Later they probably intermarried with the earlier inhabitants, as was to happen many times in the later history of this island.

One consequence of the change is that people had time to do other things besides gather food. The routine of growing plants and keeping livestock was still time consuming, but compared with the need to hunt and gather in the wild there was time to spare. As a result, for the first time in Britain structures appeared which we see as ancient monuments, but which to their builders were part of the environment of everyday life. The remains of these structures can be examined archaeologically. They also give us our first hazy glimpse of social life in the Neolithic period. There were people with the power to order large labour forces into the field to build monuments.

Opposite page Map of Neolithic and Bronze Age Dorset.

The earliest Neolithic landscape features we can recognise are known to archaeologists as causewayed camps. They are enclosed by two or three rings of banks and ditches. We call them causewayed camps because the ditches are not continuous, but have causeways left across them. The banks however, were probably continuous, except for the entrances.

There are several good examples in Dorset, all of which have to some extent been excavated. One lies under the visible remains of the Iron Age Hillfort at Maiden Castle near Dorchester, and cannot itself be seen today. Another lies on the southern end of Hambledon Hill near Child Okeford. Although this does not have a hillfort on top of it, only slight traces of it can be seen on the ground. A third (Flagstones) was partly destroyed by the building of the Dorchester by-pass and is described in the report (see Further Reading). The surviving half lies under Thomas Hardy's house at Max Gate.

In four of the ditch sections of the causewayed camp at Flagstones, not only were the marks of the antler picks used for digging still visible, but circular and criss-cross patterns had been drawn on the sides. A number of people had been buried in and around the sacred enclosure, some at the time of its construction and some many years later. Several of these had large slabs of sarsen stone covering the graves.

The most famous causewayed camp is the first to be recognised, that on Windmill Hill near Avebury in Wiltshire. This is better than the Dorset ones for a visit, as the banks and ditches have to some extent been reconstructed. The name Windmill Hill is used as a label for the distinctive style of pottery, the first to be made and used in Britain. The bowls have round bottoms, for no one had flat tables to stand them on. Identical pots were found at Hambledon and Maiden Castle.

What are these structures for? We can only look at the evidence recorded by the excavators. There is no evidence of buildings inside the camps. Almost all the finds come from the ditches, where they survive protected from the plough or other interference. And the finds are surprising. There is the evidence of feasts, including animal bones

Neolithic flint arrow heads. They are about 5cm (2 inches) long.

and broken pots. More disturbingly there are human bodies, in considerable numbers at Hambledon. Here there were also numbers of flint arrow heads, suggesting a violent attack by enemies. For the first time we have evidence of warfare.

The function of the causewayed camps is a matter of much debate. Almost certainly they were not camps used for living in, as the evidence for this would be quite different. What went on there must have been part of the tribal ritual – in fact they are the first evidence for the existence of tribes.

On certain occasions it would seem that the tribe gathered there for ceremonies which included feasting, and may well have had something to do with death, as most excavated causewayed camps have produced human bones, particularly skulls. At some sites they have been carefully buried, at others casually dumped in the ditches. It may be that the tribe gathered there for funerals, involving elaborate ceremonies including the exposure of the bodies to the point that the bones were picked clean, before they were deposited in the tribal graves which we shall consider next.

The second and most dramatic structure which characterised the Neolithic age is known today as the long barrow. Its shape distinguishes it from the round barrows of the later Bronze Age, and its function is entirely different.

Mounds of earth which can be well over 90 metres (300 feet) long, contain within them burial chambers which may be of stone or wood. If they are stone, then the chamber may not have collapsed in the five thousand years since they were built. Such chambers form the cromlechs and quoits of Wales and south-west Britain, where the soil mound has been weathered away, but the stone chamber remains. In single or multiple rooms, the bones of the dead were deposited. Broken pots in the entrances suggest elaborate burial rituals. There was no flesh on the bones when they were brought in, as they lie loose on the floor. This is why it has been suggested that the bodies were exposed for the flesh to rot away ('excarnation') in the causewayed camps.

The most spectacular examples are in Wiltshire and Gloucestershire. Best known of all is West Kennet long barrow at Avebury, which has been reconstructed. You can walk into the dark interior, an eerie experience, even though the bones have long been removed.

In Dorset over sixty long barrows have been identified. The majority had wooden interiors, which have long since rotted or were sometimes burnt down in antiquity. There are excellent examples on Pimperne Down, and at Thickthorn Down near Cranborne, lying near the south-west end of the Dorset Cursus (also a Neolithic monument). There were a few stone examples, including the Hell Stone near Portesham. The stones still stand here, and you can clamber inside. However, they are not in their original positions, having been re-erected in recent times. The map shows that the long barrows lie mostly on the chalk uplands, and in two major groupings, around and to the west of Dorchester, and along the line of the Dorset Cursus.

The end of the long barrows is equally extraordinary. After at least a thousand years of their existence, the order went out to close the

The Bank Barrow on Martins Down in West Dorset. Certainly built in the early Neolithic period, its purpose is uncertain.

tombs. This can be seen well at West Kennet long barrow, where large stone slabs weighing ten tons or more were erected across the entrance. You have to step round them to get into the tomb today. In addition, the whole of the interior was filled solid with earth, effectively sealing the tomb and bringing its use to an end. There is increasing evidence that this happened over a wide area at a roughly similar date. It must reflect a dramatic political and religious change in society. Henceforth the burial ritual changed to that of individual burial in round barrows.

Dorset has 3 rather unusual neolithic monuments which appear at first sight to be very long barrows indeed. However, no burials have been found within them, and they may have some special purpose which we do not understand. Archaeologists call them bank barrows, and they are to be found at Came Down, near Dorchester, Martin's Down, near Long Bredy, and one within Maiden Castle. The Maiden Castle example is 545 metres long (1790 feet).

By the third millennium BC there is evidence that political and religious power had spread widely across Europe. 'Megalithic' ('big stone') tombs were to be found from Orkney and Shetland to Malta and beyond. One might expect that, for example, Orkney would have been a backwater in political power at that time. Far from it. The tombs in Orkney are perhaps the most spectacular of all. Maes Howe and the stalled cairn at Mid Howe stand out as burial monuments of extraordinary engineering construction. It is not too fanciful to call the people who designed and constructed them architects.

Dorset was part of this widespread cultural identity. It's sad that these people were not literate. There are carvings on some of the tombs, but patterns rather than words.

THE DORSET CURSUS

Several long barrows are associated with perhaps the most strange of the Neolithic monuments in Dorset, the Dorset Cursus.

There are other examples in Dorset, but the famous one is a seven mile long avenue between earth banks and ditches, running between Thickthorn Down and Pentridge. It varies in width from 90 metres (300 feet) to 120 metres (400 feet), and the ditches are inside the banks. Alas, almost all of it has been ploughed away, a sad comment on the value we attach to such monuments of our past. You can only see the original size of the banks at its south-western end on Thickthorn Down, where the terminal still exists. This gives an idea of the grandeur of the original monument.

It's an awesome work, requiring many hours of labour by large groups of men, especially when you bear in mind that only stone and animal bone tools were available.

Ridiculous suggestions have been made for its purpose, including its use by flying saucers as a landing strip! In reality it must reflect an aspect of tribal ritual which we have already seen in the causewayed camps and the long barrows. It starts and ends near groups of long barrows, and on Gussage Hill the banks pass either side of a long barrow, leaving only a narrow gap. At one spot the northern bank actually runs over a long barrow from end to end.

Perhaps we should imagine elaborate processions winding their way from end to end of the sacred enclosure to celebrate in front of

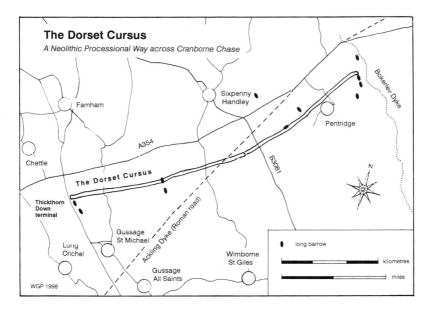

The Dorset Cursus
A Neolithic Processional Way across Cranborne Chase

Farnham

Sixpenny
Handley

Pentridge

Bokerley Dyke

A354

B3081

Chettle

The Dorset Cursus

Thickthorn
Down
terminal

Gussage
St Michael

Ackling Dyke (Roman road)

Long
Crichel

Wimborne
St Giles

long barrow

Gussage
All Saints

kilometres

miles

WGP 1998

the long barrows. But this is far from certain, and the procession would have had to climb over the banks to enter, as there are no entrances.

There is an early terminal on Wyke Down, from which the cursus was later extended further north-east. If you had stood here at midwinter about 2,500 B C and looked south-west towards Gussage Hill, the sun would have set neatly between the left hand bank of the cursus and the end of the long barrow which lies across the cursus. Such alignments can be coincidence, but they happen far too often to dismiss their importance. The knowledge of astronomy which they indicate must have been an significant part of the ritual and the power of neolithic priests.

Where did these people live? Amazingly, it is almost impossible to answer this question. They were farming, so cannot have been constantly on the move. However, they may have moved on every few years. It is not clear how soon they learnt to maintain the fertility of the soil, which was certainly happening by the end of the Bronze Age. We do not find in Britain evidence of permanent homes occupied over long periods in the Neolithic period.

Over the two thousand years of the Neolithic Age they farmed

Flint axes of the Neolithic period. These were the tools used to
clear the forests for cultivation.

large areas of Dorset, clearing for the first time the forest which had
grown after the end of the last Ice Age. Even the chalk uplands were
heavily forested at this time, and the clearance and cultivation began
the process by which much of the fertile topsoil from the hilltops has
ended in the valley bottoms.

The key to this advance lies in the development of advanced stone
axes, which were capable of felling trees. These are polished to a
high degree, and very sharp. Replicas have been made in recent times
and used successfully for this purpose. Such axes have frequently
been found in Dorset, and can be seen in the Dorset County Museum
in Dorchester. They are usually discovered by accident rather than
excavation, loose in the soil after many years of being moved about
by agriculture.

Most are made from flint mined locally, though we do not have the
spectacular flint mines of Norfolk such as Grimes Graves. However,
some are of stone which came from such places such as Langdale in
the Lake District, where you can still see hundreds of half finished or
damaged examples lying on the hillside beside what can only be
called a Neolithic axe factory.

It is clear that many of the artefacts of everyday life in Dorset were bought from itinerant traders, and this includes pottery, which was rarely made locally, as can be demonstrated by analysis of the clay.

When you see Neolithic artefacts displayed in museums, remember that, unless the circumstances are exceptional, only those made of stone or bone will have survived. Objects made of leather, wood and textiles will not appear, although they will have formed an important part of everyday living.

The polished flint axes are remarkably fine. Bone was carved with great skill, and ornament was important.

Outside Dorset, one of the most significant sites in Britain was that discovered at Skara Brae on Orkney, where a whole underground village had been buried in sand in a storm. Visit Skara Brae, and you will obtain a vivid feeling of the atmosphere of daily life in the Neolithic Age.

THE HENGE MONUMENTS

The terms Palaeolithic, Mesolithic, Neolithic, Bronze and Iron Ages are convenient labels, but there is a danger in them. It's all too easy to imagine that they are entirely separate from one another, that when the first trader landed with a bronze axe for sale, for example, everything suddenly changed and a new age began.

Of course it was not like that. Life was continuous, and changes occurred gradually. There is no real evidence of violent revolution or total reorganisation of life. Nevertheless towards the end of the Neolithic period and the beginning of the Bronze Age there were startling developments. Archaeologists sometimes call this period from about 2,500 to 1,500 BC the 'Late Neolithic – Early Bronze Age' as it needs to be seen as a whole.

What happened is often described as the growth of 'ceremonial'. There had been ceremonies before at the causewayed camps and the long barrows, but what happened now went far beyond this. Tribal identity has already been guessed at in the communal burials in the long barrows (it is unlikely that all the population was interred in them, only selected families). It is even possible that the long barrows mark tribal boundaries in some way.

But now things changed a lot. The causewayed camps were

abandoned. The long barrows were blocked up. Pottery developed into new forms, known to us a Peterborough ware. A new style of pottery appears, known as grooved ware, and this is found frequently at the new monuments that now begin to be built.

These are the henge monuments. There are none outside Britain, so we are looking at an exclusively British structure. They may well have been the direct successors to the causewayed camps. The henge at Mount Pleasant, near Dorchester, is very close to Flagstones, the existence of which was only revealed by the construction of the Dorchester by-pass.

A henge monument is a circular area surrounded by a bank with a ditch on the inside. Some have a single entrance, and others have two on opposite sides. A few are very small, even 10 metres (11 yards), while Mount Pleasant is nearly 400 metres (450 yards) across.

Occasionally the interiors are empty (as far as is known) while sometimes they contain arrangements of posts, stones or even pits. Again there is no normal domestic refuse, which suggests they were used as tribal centres for grand political or religious ceremonies.

There are often related monuments such as stone circles, avenues and ring ditches, in the near vicinity. A famous henge is at Avebury with its elaborate rows of stones, contrasting with Woodhenge, much smaller but containing an elaborate setting of wooden posts which may even have been an enormous roofed building.

The most celebrated henge of all is Stonehenge, where the elaborate stone architecture with mortise and tenon joints in dressed sarsen stones make clear the power of those who ordered its construction, and the skill of those who constructed it. There can be no doubt that much of the plan of Stonehenge reflects a deep knowledge of the movements of the moon, the sun and possibly other stars. Many other stone and timber circles in Britain show this knowledge.

They were truly remarkable people, and this was a period in our history comparable with the Industrial Revolution.

Dorchester is not left out. There is the Mount Pleasant henge, lying on the eastern outskirts of the modern town, just beyond Hardy's house at Max Gate. Since most of its interior details were in timber, they have of course rotted, leaving little visible today. Nevertheless,

Mount Pleasant near Dorchester. This is the largest of the Dorset Henge Monuments. Once its banks stood as high as those at Avebury, but now it has been ploughed almost completely flat. The aerial photograph shows clearly the enclosing bank and ditch, the enormous circular wooden structure inside, and even the thin line of the timber palisade.

even though the site has been ploughed for many years, traces of the great enclosing bank are clear to see in the chalk soil. It was partially excavated in 1970 and we know that inside the bank and ditch was an extraordinary palisade, formed of large tree trunks set 2 metres (6 feet) in the ground, almost touching, and extending all the way round the henge except for the entrances. It must have been an astonishing sight. Within the enclosure was a set of timber uprights set in circles up to 40 metres (45 yards) in diameter, in a similar way to Woodhenge.

This was undoubtedly a major tribal centre, and the size of the monument demonstrates great power and influence. What exactly went on there, we shall never know, but a glance at the ceremonial and ritual of modern day events such as a coronation or the installation of a new Archbishop of Canterbury can give us a good idea.

The Mount Pleasant henge is not the only important monument to have been found at Dorchester. Maumbury Rings on the southern edge of Dorchester is well known as the amphitheatre for the Roman

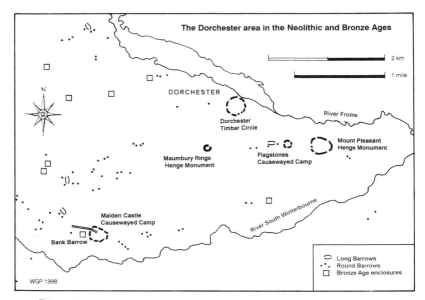

Map of the Dorchester area in the Neolithic and Bronze Age periods.

town, but in the excavations which started in 1908 it was found that the Roman engineers had remodelled a pre-existing henge monument, which just happened to be the right size. The excavators found that inside the enclosing bank a circle of deep pits had been dug in the late Neolithic period using antler picks. Their purpose is unknown, but they are similar to the 'Aubrey Holes' found at Stonehenge.

During the excavation by Wessex Archaeology in the centre of Dorchester in advance of the building of the Waitrose store, enormous timber posts, this time more widely separated, were found underlying the later Roman and medieval towns. The excavations were not extensive enough to know whether the posts formed a circle or perhaps a vast avenue leading down to the river, providing a parallel to the famous avenue at Stonehenge. In time we shall know the answer to this, but it requires digging on a large scale to locate the posts and make sense of them. In the basement level of the Waitrose car park you can still see their positions, as some of the posts are marked in red upon the floor.

There are two small stone circles to the west of Dorchester, which

[32]

The Nine Stones near Winterbourne Abbas.

may reflect on a smaller scale the functions of the large henges. One is Nine Stones near Winterbourne Abbas. The stones are sarsen, and the small circle (diameter 8 metres, 26 feet) is situated in the valley bottom right beside the stream. Two stones are much larger than the rest. Worship at these stones seems never to have stopped, as evidence of late night rituals is often to be seen. The other circle is at Kingston Russell, north of Abbotsbury, where eighteen fallen stones of conglomerate, form a tattered remnant of a once impressive small circle. It is an oval in shape, 24 metres (80 feet) by 27 metres (90 feet).

Away from Dorchester there is one other site which appears comparable in its importance at this time; this is Knowlton, which is north of Wimborne. Here, in open country there were two henges and possibly three. Around them lie many Bronze Age barrows, including an enormous one known as the Great Barrow. Only one henge has survived unploughed and is in fact the best preserved henge in Dorset. It contains a fifteenth century church which used the henge as its churchyard. The ruins of the church in its Neolithic setting create an extraordinary atmosphere.

THE FIRST METAL USERS

We have seen how the major henges were constructed in the period from 2,500 to 1,500 BC. It is over roughly the same period that equally startling changes occur in burial practices, and the first appearance of metal artefacts occurs. We use the label Bronze Age, but the details of what happened are more complex than this suggests.

The great long barrows were ceremonially closed down, and the practice of individual burial under round barrows became normal. In addition cremation became gradually more popular. This implies a change of religion, perhaps the same events that caused the building of the great henges. The new order was persuasive, or backed by political power. It takes a lot to change such habits in a human community. We must be looking at an edict from central authority.

In terms of archaeology the round barrows have produced some of the most celebrated excavations in modern times, since some of them contain golden grave goods. The earliest round barrows contained inhumations (i.e. burials), but later, cremations were more common. This again reflects a major change in people's beliefs.

The first round barrows were built about 2,700 BC and these usually contained inhumations accompanied by 'beakers'. This has been one the most fascinating debates of prehistoric studies in recent years. These large jars, shaped rather like an upturned bell, are so distinctive that their owners have been called the 'beaker folk', and their arrival taken to indicate a violent invasion. Some investigators even imagined they could identify beaker folk by the shape of their heads, though this is no longer accepted.

As we have seen, an invasion did not necessarily happen, although it remains a possibility. It is marginally more likely that the beakers arrived by way of trade, perhaps with food contents of some sort, or to satisfy the need for beer mugs to use with a new fad in strong drink – could it have been mead?! Traces of mead have been identified in a specimen from Scotland. The earliest beakers were made in the Rhineland, and were only later imitated in Britain. It is this fact which leaves open the possibility that the beakers arrived with a group of new immigrants, whose power and influence was such as to cause the large changes in public and private life. The debate about beakers will go on for many years yet.

Some of these same beaker barrows contain the first metal to be found in Britain. Daggers are found in the graves, clearly a symbol of the personal wealth and power of the deceased. The very earliest ones are of copper, but soon these are replaced by bronze, the alloy of copper and tin. Bronze had already been made in the Middle East for centuries before it appeared in Britain. While copper is generally too soft for tools, mixing it with tin produces a much harder material which is suitable for tools and weapons, as well as an adornment when suitably polished to a high degree of brightness.

Bronze was the first metal used in any quantity, mainly because of the easy availability of the ores concerned (though not in Dorset) and the comparatively low temperature at which they melt. The development of iron had to await a technique of raising rather higher temperatures. Most of the bronze tools found in the barrows were

Two beakers from Dorset barrows of the early Bronze Age.

produced by pouring the metal into moulds, which have themselves occasionally been found.

From the very beginning, a small number of barrows contained gold items as the ultimate status symbol. Gold is the easiest of all metals to work, but the most difficult to find. The gold in the round barrows came from Ireland and possibly from South Wales and Scotland.

This has had a near-disastrous effect in archaeological terms. Once it became known in the nineteenth century that gold was a possibility, wealthy landowners and their parsons began to dig systematically in barrows on their land with the hope of finding treasure. Although some, such as Richard Colt-Hoare of Stourhead, were responsible diggers and published their results and placed the finds on display in their houses or specially built museums, many more treasure hunters were happy to conceal their finds and melt down the gold for sale.

We have lost untold information about the Bronze Age this way, and it is rare to find a round barrow that has not had its central burial tunnelled into for treasure without regard for all the other archaeological information it contains.

The study of the Bronze Age depends upon the round barrows. If we did not have these we would know next to nothing about the people of this period. On the other hand it must be remembered that we only see them when they are dead, and we have only a partial view. It is rather like studying recent history through the monuments in twentieth century cemeteries.

We are dealing with a long period, from the earliest beaker barrows in the mid-third millennium, to the latest examples in the early first millennium. There are considerable changes, though the central principle of a round shaped mound over a inhumation, or later cremation, continues.

A glance at the map on page 20 of Dorset in the Neolithic and Bronze Age periods, shows that the round barrows occur in large numbers across Dorset. Often they cluster round groups of Neolithic long barrows, as near the Dorset Cursus. It is estimated that Dorset had upwards of 2,000 round barrows. They occur almost everywhere, but the main concentrations lie south-west to north-east on

The Bronze Age barrow cemetery at Poor Lot, near Winterbourne Abbas.

the upland chalk, where settlement seems to have been most dense.

Some barrows continued in use for centuries, for following the original central burial, other members of the family were later buried elsewhere in the mound. Either it was important to be near the first burial, or it may even have saved building another mound, a considerable task. Sometimes, as at the Fordington Barrow in Dorchester, this involved the digging of a new and wider ditch, and the erection of an even larger mound.

By the very last years of the Bronze Age there are mounds with as many as a hundred pots containing ashes, while other mounds are surrounded by cemeteries spreading over a considerable area, where the burials are made without individual mounds at all. It is likely that this reflects a rising population brought about by settled agriculture. Archaeologists call this period 'Deverel-Rimbury', named partly after the Deverel barrow in Milborne St. Andrew, where more than twenty urns were found.

Wessex (mainly Dorset and Wiltshire) was at the centre of round barrow building. Along the South Dorset Ridgeway for example, there are at least 400 round barrows still to be seen, and many more ploughed over.

However, all is not lost after ploughing, as the original ('primary') burial was below the ancient ground surface, and may still survive. Certainly the barrow may still appear on aerial photographs. Nearly all had a ditch round the outside (mainly to provide the material for the mound) and the fill of this buried ditch will be visible in suitable conditions.

Among the barrows of Wessex were some with very rich objects indeed. It is tempting to think that buried in these barrows were the elite of Bronze Age Wessex, perhaps the very leaders who had the power to bring about the building of Mount Pleasant and Stonehenge.

No one is at all certain whether the great henges were built by armies of slaves, or by people inspired by religious fervour. But in either case there will have been powerful kings or priests behind the projects.

One of the richest burials, which might well be associated with the monuments at Dorchester, is the Clandon Barrow at Martinstown.

Clandon was dug in 1882. The ashes of the original burial were not found, but there was a grooved bronze dagger, a quadrangular gold plate, a shale mace head with gold discs, an incense cup, and a cup made of amber. These surely represent the symbols of office of a chief of some sort. They can be seen in Dorset County Museum. The Bush Barrow in Wiltshire had a similar gold plate, and its finds can be seen at the Museum in Devizes.

It is not clear to what extent these exotic artefacts were made in Britain, or imported as valuable presents. In any case the amber had to come from Scandinavia, gold from Ireland, and the polished stone from highland parts of Britain.

There is a wide variety of barrow shapes, again mainly in Wessex. The rich ones are usually ordinary 'bowl' barrows, but there are bowl barrows, bell barrows, disc barrows, saucer barrows and pond barrows. The pond barrows, of which there is a splendid example in Came Wood near Dorchester, are a puzzle. All the others have a mound of some sort, but pond barrows are simply a hollow with the burials in the bottom. Came Wood and the adjacent fields contains a typical barrow cemetery with bowl barrows, bell barrows and pond barrows. They stretch in a long line and seem to be roughly aligned on a large bank barrow, probably belonging to the Neolithic, though this is not proved.

At Oakley Down near Sixpenny Handley there is another large cemetery, including three large disc barrows, one of which contains two burial mounds arranged symmetrically. At Poor Lot near Winterbourne Abbas a cemetery is unusually sited in a valley bottom.

The interesting details of round barrows are endless. The question

The Clandon Barrow near Dorchester, burial site of a 'Wessex Chieftain'. In this barrow were found the spectacular items shown on the back cover. The aerial photograph shows traces of other ploughed out barrows in the vicinity.

which cannot at present be answered, is whether all the population received this elaborate treatment, or only selected families. If not all, then where are the others? No other form of burial is found for this period. If the barrows cover all the population, even allowing for lost barrows, then there are comparatively few people, and it is even more surprising that so many people could be assembled to build Mount Pleasant and Stonehenge.

Although at first the bronze artefacts appear only as prized personal possessions in the barrows, as the Bronze Age progressed bronze axes and spearheads became used more widely. This is shown by the fact that they are sometimes found casually in the fields, where they were accidentally lost while being used. Occasionally hoards are found, including worn out specimens, suggesting that they belonged to travelling bronze smiths. By the end of the Bronze Age it is clear that such tools were in everyday use. Nevertheless flint was still widely used, and flint tools found in the fields today are as likely to have been made in the Bronze Age as in earlier periods.

Dorset County Museum holds a wide variety of Bronze Age pots. We are of course seeing the pots used for cremations and burials, and it is not clear if the same range would have been used in everyday life. Perhaps the large urns containing ashes were also used to store grain, or perhaps they were made specially for burials.

THE LATE BRONZE AGE LANDSCAPE

After about 1,000 BC it becomes possible for us to see traces of permanent fields and settlement sites. This may be associated with an increase of the population in the middle of the second millennium, and a consequent expansion of agriculture and the need to keep the soil fertile and settle in permanent farms. If there are many more people in existence, finding new land to cultivate by simply moving

Opposite page Bronze Age artefacts from Dorset include the urns in which the ashes of the dead were deposited in the round barrows. Amongst other objects found in the county are two forms of axe, a spear head, and a fine dagger with a reconstructed bone handle.

The Bronze Age barrow cemetery at Oakley Down, near Sixpenny Handley.
This contains four disc barrows, circular enclosures with small burial
mounds within them. In the foreground the Roman road just clips
the edge of one of the disc barrows.

on, becomes much more difficult. The abandonment of the formal
round barrow burials also supports this assumption.

The pattern of ancient fields on the landscape is a common sight on
aerial photographs. Much of Dorset was eventually covered in these
small fields, especially the chalk uplands. It is more difficult to know
what happened in the valleys because of more intensive later occupation, and soil washed down from the hills which may have buried
ancient settlement sites.

These fields are known to archaeologists as 'Celtic fields'. They
represent a type of cultivation which was in use from the late Bronze
Age through to the end of the Roman period, at least 1,400 years.
They were not ploughed with the mouldboard plough of today or
even the medieval model. They were broken up with the ard, which
was simply a spike hauled through the ground by oxen. The weeds
were not buried, so the farmer had to use hoes and rakes to knock

the weeds out of the soil, and gather them up and burn them. The whole process is described by Roman writers such as Varro and Columella. And very hard work it sounds too.

A majority of the Celtic fields we can still see today belong to the Iron Age and Roman periods, when the population was very much higher again, and much of the upland chalk was cultivated. But in some places the earliest groups of fields go back to the Bronze Age when permanent agriculture was initially developed.

One of the first places to be recognised as dating from the Bronze Age is Shearplace Hill, north of Dorchester, where a small group of fields are divided by a lane which leads to a small enclosure, containing a possible building. This site was in use in about 1,000 BC.

During the excavation by Wessex Archaeology of sites on the Western Link of the Dorchester by-pass, two circular huts were found (structures 5195 and 5196). They belonged to the Bronze Age and lynchets associated with them proved that permanent agriculture was in progress here in Fordington Bottom soon after 1,000 BC. (Lynchets are banks formed on sloping ground by the slippage of soil down the hill during continued cultivation.)

All the huts in Dorset were of timber and have left little trace. To get the feel of a late Bronze Age village visit Grimspound on Dartmoor. There it is possible to see the 16 small stone structures clearly, even without excavation. They are enclosed by a wall of stone boulders. It is not likely that cereals could be grown here, and they must have been farming with animals. A stream passes through the site. It is even possible that they were already mining the tin on the moor, and obtaining other food by barter.

Some Celtic fields can be proved to belong to the Bronze Age simply because they carefully avoid groups of round barrows. Other barrows occur on ground which has been cultivated, but has clearly gone out of cultivation.

Britain, including Dorset, had begun to have the look of a settled agricultural landscape.

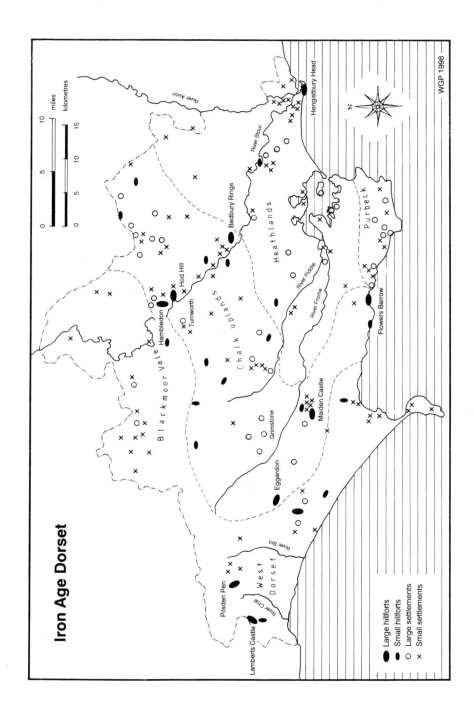

Iron Age Dorset

River Avon

River Stour

Hengistbury Head

Heathlands

Purbeck

River Piddle

River Frome

Flowers Barrow

Badbury Rings

Hod Hill

Hambledon

Turnworth

Chalk uplands

Blackmoor Vale

Maiden Castle

Grimstone

Eggardon

West Dorset

River Brit

Plisden Pen

River Char

Lamberts Castle

N

WGP 1998

miles
0   5   10

0   5   10   15
kilometres

● Large hillforts
⬭ Small hillforts
○ Large settlements
× Small settlements

THE NEW IRON TECHNOLOGY

THE COMING OF IRON

At some time in the eighth century B C iron tools began to appear in southern Britain, and the period from then to the Roman invasion is called the Iron Age.

Iron had been smelted from iron ore at least a thousand years before in the Middle East – the Hittites had used iron weapons. Its toughness gave it a great advantage over bronze for uses where strength was required, in weapons and farming equipment particularly. Its production was not easy. A temperature of 1,100 degrees Celsius will liquefy bronze completely so that it can be poured into moulds, though even this requires a forced draft and carefully constructed furnaces. But even at such temperatures iron ore will only partially melt, becoming a 'bloom' of metal mixed with ash and slag, which has to be reheated and beaten by a blacksmith to make wrought iron.

It was not until the fifteenth century in Europe that furnaces with bellows driven by water wheels were able to melt the iron completely and produce cast iron. Curiously cast iron had been made long before in China, but their ore was of a type which had a lower melting point. Their problem was to convert the rigid cast iron into a flexible metal needed for weapons.

In the first millennium B C there is rather more evidence for an influx of new people than there was for previous changes such as the arrival of beakers. Not only do iron tools appear, but the earliest Iron Age pottery is very different from the later Bronze Age types, and it is likely that at this point newcomers brought the Celtic language, which was almost universal in Britain by the Roman conquest.

From about 800 B C there is much evidence for developing trade, some of it across the Channel. Salt, essential for the preservation of food, was being produced from sea water at many places along the south coast of Dorset. Kimmeridge shale from Dorset, which had already made an appearance in barrows of the Bronze Age, now became carved into bracelets and pendants at several sites in Purbeck, including Eldon's Seat. Tin and copper mining was extended in Cornwall and Wales. Before long iron itself began to be smelted in the Weald of Kent.

Bronze was being imported from the continent, and at Langdon Bay near Dover a wrecked ship was found containing many bronze implements and much scrap metal. Recycling of the metal was the rule, indicating that it was still an expensive item.

As early as 700 BC the hilltop fortifications which are so characteristic of the Iron Age began to appear. The earliest one in Dorset may be Chalbury (perhaps 600 BC). This lies on a small hill east of Weymouth, near the villages of Preston and Sutton Poyntz. It is an important site for the understanding of the early Iron Age, particularly as it perches on a steep hill. As a result it has never been ploughed. Vertical stone slabs which formed the face of its ramparts still stick out of the turf in places, and the small level terraces on which the circular huts stood are still clear to see. There was one entrance, in the south-east corner.

It was excavated in 1939 and revealed a wide range of pottery belonging to the early Iron Age. There are large jars with vertical rims for storing grain, and fine dishes coated with red haematite for table use (most pots now have flat bottoms, suggesting that flat surfaces existed to put them on). This class of pottery is known to archaeologists as 'Iron Age A'.

In Dorset generally there was clearly pressure on land. In addition to the new hilltop fortified settlements, farms and villages appeared and new areas of Celtic fields were developed. By the end of the Iron Age it is commonly supposed that the population of southern Britain was as much as a million. Certainly new fields were taken into cultivation down the sides of hills where it was awkward to plough. There is scarcely a parish in Dorset which does not contain Iron Age fields and farms, either as surviving earthworks, or as crop marks on aerial photographs. The most intensive occupation was on the chalk uplands, which seems to have been the case for most of prehistory. This does not of course preclude some settlement on the heathlands

A small early Iron Age Hillfort at Chalbury, near Weymouth. There is one entrance in the lower right hand corner. The interior has never been ploughed, and the foundations of the huts of the inhabitants can be clearly seen.

An early Iron Age Hillfort at Abbotsbury Castle. The eleven houses it contained can be seen on the far side of the enclosure.

Reconstruction of an Iron Age hut at the New Barn Field Centre,
Bradford Peverell.

and in valley bottoms, but these were much less numerous.

The classic site where an Iron Age farm was first excavated and understood was at Little Woodbury in Wiltshire in 1938. What was probably an extended family lived in a very large house indeed. It was circular in shape, measuring 15 metres (17 yards) across. A house of this size needed two rings of posts to support the conical thatched roof. A fire burned, probably night and day, in the middle, and with the doors closed it would have been a comfortable home.

Modern families lived in such a house in the experiment conducted at Rushmore in Dorset for the BBC programme 'Living in the Past'. While the programme concentrated on the relationships of the people involved in the experiment, a great deal was learned about how life would have been lived in such a community.

Reconstructions of Iron Age round houses can be seen today at a number of sites, notably at Butser near Petersfield in Hampshire, and in Dorset at New Barn, Bradford Peverell, west of Dorchester. At a site next to Cranborne School there is another Iron Age village reconstruction with a programme of experiments into life in the Iron

Age. Butser and New Barn are open to the public, but an appointment is needed at Cranborne.

One of the commonest features found on Iron Age sites is the grain storage pit. Before Sir Mortimer Wheeler's excavations at Maiden Castle in 1935, the deep pits seen on Iron Age sites were thought by many to be pit dwellings. This was because domestic rubbish was often found in them. But in the British climate, which in the first millennium BC became similar to that of today, such homes would frequently fill with water!

It is now realised that the pits were lined with wickerwork and clay, and used to store grain. Experiments at Butser have demonstrated the practicability of this method of storage, odd though it seems to us. It is possible that storage in this form could be camouflaged, and your store of food might survive a hostile attack.

There are two excellent sites in Dorset where small Iron Age villages have, by historical accident, not been ploughed, and the visitor can walk the ancient lanes through the fields to the village. The first is at Grimstone (see Places to Visit) four miles north-west of Dorchester. The village centre is surrounded by its Celtic fields, and a

The Iron Age farming landscape: at Grimstone near Dorchester the low sun picks out the small 'Celtic' fields of the village which lies in front of the wood.

The Iron Age landscape: at Turnworth in North Dorset a circular ditch and bank encloses a farm, around which lie its fields and lanes. Like Grimstone it was still in use in Roman times.

lane leads through the fields till it comes out on what was probably common land in the valley bottom. The second is at Turnworth in north Dorset, where a similar pattern exists.

All the known Iron Age villages in Dorset were on comparatively high ground, and as the population rose new fields were cleared down the hillsides. This is the exact opposite to the situation in medieval times, when the village centres were in the valley bottom, and new furlong strips necessarily climbed up the hillsides. At Plush near Piddletrenthide the two systems can be seen overlapping.

THE HILLFORTS

An early hillfort like Chalbury was a modest affair, providing protection for its inhabitants, a family group or tribe. Threats must have existed, and given the nature of the human race this is no surprise. It may well be that the constantly increasing population was a signifi-cant cause of the development of warfare. But later in the Iron

Age, especially in the first two centuries BC, hillforts expanded both in number and size. A majority were expansions of existing early hillforts. The single rampart became two, three or even four. The method of construction of ramparts changed.

The early hillforts had 'box' ramparts, as at Chalbury. A vertical back and front made of timber uprights and dry stone infill contained a rubble core. This was a sophisticated method of construction, the knowledge of which had come from the continent. The later ramparts were of the 'glacis' type, where the earth was merely piled as steep as possible, the sloping line being carried straight down into the ditch. These were much easier to construct and maintain, as the only timber was in the palisade at the top, providing cover for the defenders.

This is what is seen at Maiden Castle today, though Wheeler's excavation showed that originally it had the single box rampart of the early type. Looking at Maiden Castle, it is hard to imagine it newly constructed, when all the banks were gleaming white chalk.

If you walk the ploughed fields below Maiden Castle, particularly at the eastern end, you may be surprised to see large pebbles that originated on Chesil Beach. Wheeler found large dumps of them inside the ramparts, and there is no doubt what they were for. The long distance weapon which the Durotriges fired from the ramparts, was the sling, and the pebbles were the ammunition. Even hillforts as far away from the coast as South Cadbury Castle (in Somerset, but still in Durotrigian territory) had Chesil Beach pebbles stacked behind the ramparts. It is tempting to imagine the families living in Abbotsbury Castle making a living by trading the pebbles round the hillforts, but there is no proof of this of course.

The best place to study the construction of ramparts is on the south side of Maiden Castle. Here the job was never finished properly, and you can see the half built ramparts. Each ditch has been started at the foot of the appropriate rampart, but only a few basketfuls have been carried to form the next rampart down before the job was abandoned.

This raises one of the major questions about hillforts. In what context were they built? Were the multiple ramparts strictly necessary to resist major threats? At the present time most archaeologists

The Iron Age Hillfort at Maiden Castle near Dorchester from the north-west.

believe the answer is no. They represent the growing dominance of tribal leaders, and are a demonstration of their power. When their greatest test came they were found wanting; they could not resist the sophisticated siege techniques of the Roman army in 43 AD.

THE DUROTRIGES

As we approach the time of the Roman conquest, the light of history begins to glow, if dimly at first. Through Roman geographers and other writers we begin to discover the actual names of the tribes whose great hillforts dominated the landscape. It is an exciting moment.

In what we now call Dorset, it is certain that the native tribe was